Teen Nonfiction - PORTR-KOU
324.273 CASTI
Castillo, Kristina C.
Political parties : division a
33410018294837   01-05-2023

CHALLENGES FOR DEMOCRACY

Political Parties: Division and Distrust

Kristina Castillo

San Diego, CA

About the Author

Kristina Castillo is a writer originally from South Carolina. She writes books for children and teens.

© 2023 ReferencePoint Press, Inc.
Printed in the United States

For more information, contact:
ReferencePoint Press, Inc.
PO Box 27779
San Diego, CA 92198
www.ReferencePointPress.com

ALL RIGHTS RESERVED.
No part of this work covered by the copyright hereon may be reproduced or used in any form or by any means—graphic, electronic, or mechanical, including photocopying, recording, taping, web distribution, or information storage retrieval systems—without the written permission of the publisher.

Picture Credits:
Cover: mark reinstein/Shutterstock Images (top left); mark reinstein/Shutterstock Images (top right); Christos Georghiou/Shutterstock Images (bottom)

4: Maury Aaseng
6: Sipa USA/Alamy Stock Photo
10: Lou Linwei/Alamy Stock Photo
13: Jeffrey Isaac Greenberg 11+/Alamy Stock Photo
17: Prostock-studio/Shutterstock Images
19: Sterling Munksgard/Shutterstock Images
22: Cindy Brown/Alamy Stock Photo
25: Tribune Content Agency LLC/Alamy Stock Photo
29: Michael Dresser/TNS/Newscom
33: Ann E Parry/Alamy Stock Photo
35: Jeff Malet Photography/Newscom
39: lev radin/Shutterstock Images
42: UPI/Alamy Stock Photo
46: stockpexel/Shutterstock Images
49: Sid Hastings/Alamy Stock Photo
52: Oleksii Arseniuk/Shutterstock Images
55: Patti McConville/Alamy Stock Photo

LIBRARY OF CONGRESS CATALOGING-IN-PUBLICATION DATA

Names: Castillo, Kristina C., author.
Title: Political parties : division and distrust / By Kristina Castillo.
Description: San Diego, CA : ReferencePoint Press, Inc., 2022. | Series: Challenges for democracy | Includes bibliographical references and index.
Identifiers: LCCN 2022014068 (print) | LCCN 2022014069 (ebook) | ISBN 9781678203061 (library binding) | ISBN 9781678203078 (ebook)
Subjects: LCSH: Political parties--Juvenile literature. | Elections--United States--Juvenile literature. | United States--Politics and government--Juvenile literature.
Classification: LCC JF2051 .C357 2022 (print) | LCC JF2051 (ebook) | DDC 324.273--dc23/eng/20220427
LC record available at https://lccn.loc.gov/2022014068
LC ebook record available at https://lccn.loc.gov/2022014069

CONTENTS

Introduction   5
The Pandemic Highlights a Divided Nation

Chapter One   9
Political Parties in the United States

Chapter Two   18
Political Parties and Elections

Chapter Three   28
Gerrymandering to Create Election Advantage

Chapter Four   38
Hyperpartisanship Threatens Democracy

Chapter Five   48
Reducing Polarization Between Parties and People

Source Notes   57
For Further Research   60
Index   62

Young Americans Have Low Opinion of US Democracy

American democracy has been experiencing many challenges. Foremost among those challenges is the widespread perception that US democracy is either "in trouble" or "failing." This is the view of a majority of young Americans, age eighteen to twenty-nine. A national poll conducted in Fall 2021 by the Harvard Kennedy School Institute of Politics finds that only 7 percent of young adults view the United States as a "healthy democracy."

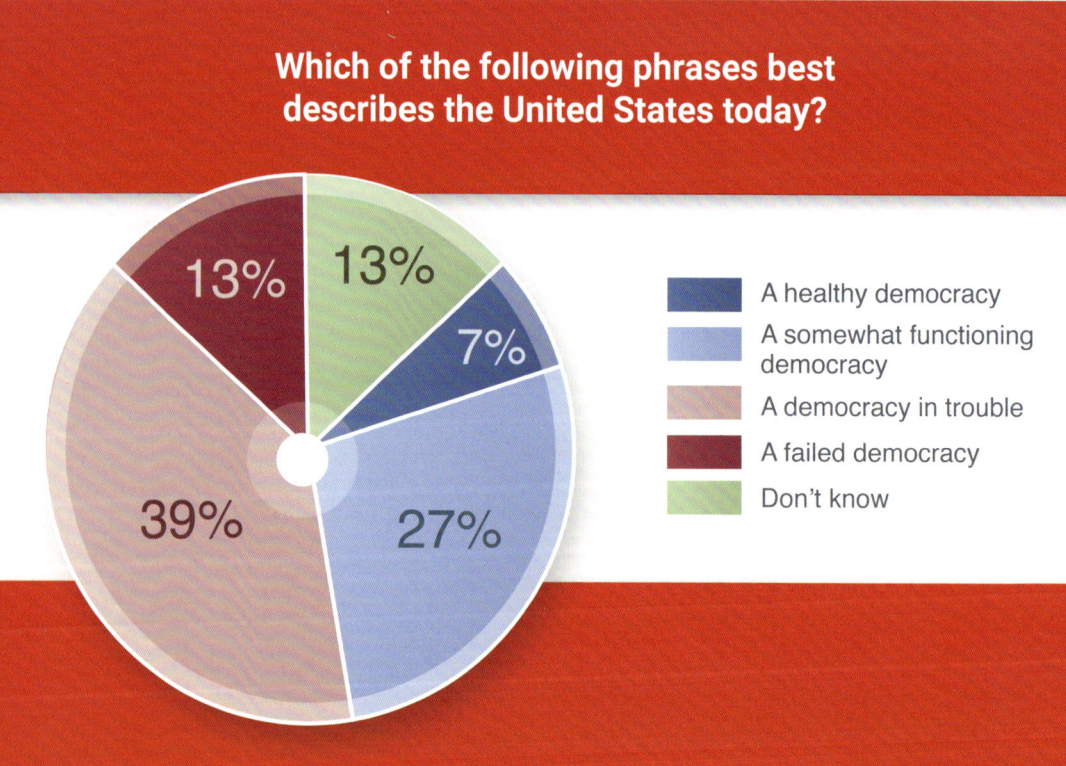

Which of the following phrases best describes the United States today?

- A healthy democracy: 7%
- A somewhat functioning democracy: 27%
- A democracy in trouble: 39%
- A failed democracy: 13%
- Don't know: 13%

Source: "Harvard Youth Poll," Harvard Kennedy School Institute of Politics, December 1, 2021. https://iop.harvard.edu.

INTRODUCTION

The Pandemic Highlights a Divided Nation

On March 11, 2020, the World Health Organization declared the COVID-19 outbreak a global pandemic. That evening, President Donald Trump gave a prime-time address from the Oval Office on the pandemic. He announced a travel ban from Europe as well as other measures being considered. At the end of the speech, he called for Americans to unify to face this public health challenge:

> We are all in this together. We must put politics aside, stop the partisanship and unify together as one nation and one family.
>
> As history has proven time and time again, Americans always rise to the challenge and overcome adversity.
>
> Our future remains brighter than anyone can imagine. Acting with compassion and love, we will heal the sick, care for those in need, help our fellow citizens and emerge from this challenge stronger and more unified than ever before.[1]

The pandemic could have brought Americans together to fight against a common enemy: a virus. After all, the nation has united against enemies throughout history, such as after the December

7, 1941 Japanese attack on Pearl Harbor and the September 11, 2001 terrorist attacks. In a display of unity hours after the September 11 attacks in New York and Washington, DC, members of Congress from both parties joined together on the Capitol steps and sang "God Bless America."

The nation's response to the pandemic stood in stark contrast to past crises and to Trump's initial call for unity. As the virus spread, many political leaders—including the president—spread misinformation about the seriousness of the pandemic, criticized government scientists, and mocked restrictions recommended by infectious disease experts. These actions widened already deep divisions. Americans became divided about COVID-19, the

Travelers arrive at a Florida airport in May 2021. During the COVID-19 pandemic, many Americans have followed the advice of health experts to wear masks and get vaccinated, but others have rejected that advice. Rather than uniting against a common enemy, Americans became more divided than ever.

restrictions aimed at slowing the spread of the virus, and the vaccines developed to keep people from getting seriously ill and dying. Some Americans relied on the advice of scientists, doctors, and public health experts, whereas other Americans rejected such advice. Conspiracy theories circulated on social media, further fueling the divide.

Party Affiliation Impacts Pandemic Opinions

The differences in opinion closely aligned with political party affiliation. In fact, party affiliation has been the strongest predictor of people's COVID-19-related behaviors and attitudes, according to a 2020 Brookings Institution study. The nonprofit public policy organization found that in 2020 Democrats were more worried about COVID-19 and were more likely to wear masks and practice social distancing than Republicans were. For example, although equal percentages of Republicans and Democrats were almost always social distancing in April 2020, by late July 2020, only 40 percent of Republicans were social distancing, whereas almost 100 percent of Democrats were doing so. In fact, party affiliation affected those behaviors and attitudes more than community infection rates or demographic characteristics such as age and health status.

Attitudes toward COVID-19 vaccines are a stark example of the divisions between the two parties. In June 2021 Harvard University analyzed vaccine data by congressional district. The study found that congressional districts with high vaccination rates were largely represented by Democrats, whereas those with low vaccination rates were represented by Republicans.

The differences in opinions and behaviors had serious consequences for public health and the economy. For instance, the Brookings Institution study found that stay-at-home orders and mask mandates—which were more prevalent in states won by Democratic presidential candidate Hillary Clinton in 2016—slowed the spread of the virus and prevented a significant number of deaths in 2020. However, harsher restrictions often produced economic harm. States with more restrictions, such as stay-at-home orders and the closure of nonessential businesses—mostly states Clinton won in 2016—suffered more economic harm than states with fewer restrictions, which were largely states that Republican presidential candidate Trump won in 2016.

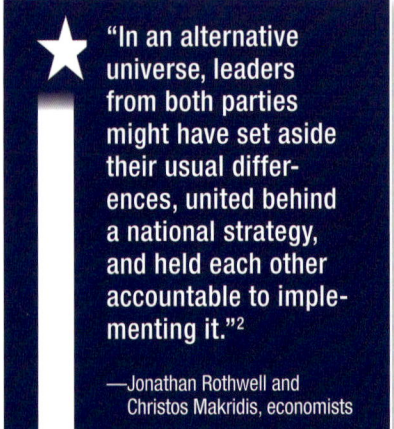

"In an alternative universe, leaders from both parties might have set aside their usual differences, united behind a national strategy, and held each other accountable to implementing it."[2]

—Jonathan Rothwell and Christos Makridis, economists

Politicians Fuel Divisiveness During Pandemic

Politicians have turned the pandemic into a divisive political issue. Instead of prioritizing the health and safety of their constituents—and the nation as a whole—many elected officials used pandemic-related press conferences and tweets to appeal to party regulars and to boost their own political careers. "In an alternative universe," economists Jonathan Rothwell and Christos Makridis write, "leaders from both parties might have set aside their usual differences, united behind a national strategy, and held each other accountable to implementing it."[2] Instead, Democrats and Republicans are further apart than ever.

As the pandemic continues, and as other serious challenges to America's way of life arise, the division between America's political parties seems to grow wider. The distrust between members of both parties seems greater than ever, which poses tremendous challenges for US democracy.

CHAPTER ONE

Political Parties in the United States

Many people assume that the system of two major political parties—the two-party system—in the United States is required by the Constitution, but it is not. When the nation was founded, the drafters of the Constitution did not include any language about political parties. That omission was intentional.

Political parties were not mentioned in the Constitution because its drafters feared political parties and their impact on democracy. For example, Alexander Hamilton once referred to political parties as the "most fatal disease."[3] John Adams warned that "a division of the republic into two great parties . . . is to be dreaded as the great political evil."[4] These fears stemmed from a belief that political parties would divide the new nation, which many of the drafters had fought for in the American Revolutionary War. The new nation was designed as a republican form of government, where the power to govern is held by the people and the representatives they elect. Many of the drafters also believed that political parties would place their own interests over those of the people, which would undermine democratic ideals.

Despite their fears, during the ratification of the Constitution, two sides formed: the Federalists and the Anti-Federalists.

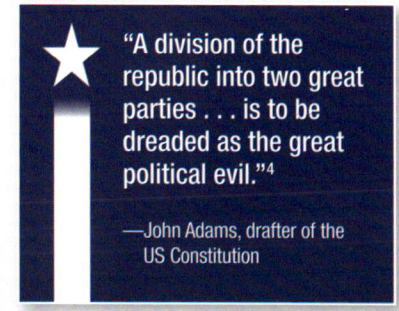

"A division of the republic into two great parties . . . is to be dreaded as the great political evil."[4]

—John Adams, drafter of the US Constitution

The Federalists supported the Constitution and a strong national government. The Anti-Federalists opposed the Constitution and favored placing power in state governments. Although these were not political parties in the formal sense, they set the stage for divisions of people based on political ideology.

The Emergence of Two Political Parties

Shortly after the nation's founding, two political parties emerged during President George Washington's administration. Due to disagreements over whether to establish a national bank and other issues, the Federalists and the Democratic-Republican Party formed. In his 1796 farewell address as president, George Washington warned about the danger of political parties. He believed they would divide the people in a young nation that needed to be unified to succeed. In that address, Washington noted that political parties could serve a purpose, but he worried that they would eventually become more powerful than the people: "However [political parties] may now and then answer popular ends, they are likely, in the course of time and things, to become potent engines by which cunning, ambitious, and unprincipled men will be enabled to subvert the power of the people and to usurp for themselves the reins of government, destroying afterwards the very engines which have lifted them to unjust dominion."[5]

In his 1796 farewell address as president, George Washington warned about the dangers of political parties. He believed that unity was essential in such a young nation, and he feared that political parties would sow division.

Third Parties and Independents

Although the United States is a two-party system, third parties also exist. Third parties generally seek to advance a particular agenda that is not actively being promoted by one of the two major parties. Some prominent third parties are the Libertarian Party and the Green Party. The Libertarian Party believes in limiting the role of the government, while the Green Party focuses on the environment and social justice.

Members of third parties have been elected to public office. However, at the national level, third-party candidates are rarely successful. Nevertheless, third parties can affect government in ways outside of securing elective office. For example, the principles espoused by third-party candidates may end up being absorbed by one of the two major parties, and thus they can serve a role in advancing or changing policy.

In contrast to third parties, independents are people who are not affiliated with any political party. According to a 2021 Gallup poll, more Americans (42 percent) identify as independents than as Democrats (29 percent) or Republicans (27 percent). Both parties fight to win votes from independents, particularly in tight races.

Despite Washington's concerns, Americans embraced the two-party system that has dominated the nation's politics ever since. Although the names and values of the parties have changed, the two political parties are powerful forces in the nation's political life and government. The two major parties are the Democratic Party and the Republican Party. In every US presidential election since 1852 except one, candidates from the Democratic and Republican parties have placed first and second.

What Are Political Parties?

Political parties are organizations of people who share common ideas about how a country (or state or city) should be governed. Their members include voters, candidates, elected officials, and party leaders who are unified by guiding principles. Political parties work to advance those principles by creating a party platform and nominating and supporting candidates for elective office. The major goals of political parties include winning elections and holding political power. To meet these goals, they nominate candidates they believe will win elections, fund-raise for their candidates, and communicate with the public about their candidates.

Parties also work to transform the interests of their members into policies, which they seek to enact. When a political party has a large number of its members in elective offices, the party can usually advance its desired policies. For example, parties draft bills and pressure their members in legislatures to introduce those bills and work to pass them. When a party is in control of a legislative body—meaning that it has more members than the opposing party—the controlling party can usually succeed in passing its bills into laws. Unlike interest groups that influence the policy-making process to serve the interests of one group or one cause, political parties aim to promote a comprehensive policy agenda that serves a large population.

Most democratic countries have political parties. Many democratic countries have a multiparty system, meaning that they have numerous political parties that have an opportunity to gain control of the government. The United States has a two-party system, which means that one of two major parties—either the Democratic or Republican Party—controls the government at any given time.

People can register their political party affiliation when registering to vote. Each state has its own rules for how to register to vote. Voters can change their political party affiliation by updating their voter registration. A voter without a party affiliation is known as an independent.

Political Parties Can Promote Democratic Values

Political parties perform many functions that promote democratic values. As Jennifer Victor, a political science professor at George Mason University, explains, "Parties are important for a healthy democracy because they help solve problems for voters, candidates, and elected officials that these groups are unable to solve on their own."[6] For example, parties help candidates raise money and campaign, which are difficult for most candidates to do on their own.

A Republican Party volunteer helps with a voter registration drive in Miami, Florida. Political parties encourage citizen participation in the democratic process through voter registration drives and other activities.

Parties encourage participation in the democratic process at all levels. Specifically, parties educate people about running for office at the local, state, and national levels. They encourage people to register to vote by sending reminders via mail, email, or social media as well as through in-person voter registration drives. They also inform voters about the candidates running for elective office. In many states, volunteers from political parties act as poll watchers on Election Day, observing the voting process to ensure that everything is running smoothly and in compliance with election laws. Party volunteers may also drive people who lack transportation to the polls to vote. After Election Day, political parties organize caucuses or coalitions—groups that work together toward a common goal—in legislative bodies so that government can function and pass laws. This happens in state legislatures as well as in Congress.

> "Parties are important for a healthy democracy because they help solve problems for voters, candidates, and elected officials that these groups are unable to solve on their own."[6]
>
> —Jennifer Victor, political science professor at George Mason University

Party Platforms

A party platform is a statement of what the party plans to do if it wins a given election. In 2020 the Democratic Party adopted a platform that addressed issues related to health care, the economy, climate change, and criminal justice. The 2020 platform supported a public health insurance option for all Americans, investments in clean energy, a path to citizenship for unauthorized immigrants, and changes to the criminal justice system. The platform also proposed free college tuition for students whose families earn less than $125,000 a year.

In 2020 the Republican Party chose not to update its 2016 party platform. Instead, the party stated it would continue its support for the policies of the Trump administration. This included trade restrictions, reduced immigration, and construction of a wall along the US-Mexico border. The 2016 platform opposed same-sex marriage and transgender rights, specifically criticizing guidance from the US Department of Education allowing students to use restrooms that conform with their gender identity. It also encouraged states to offer elective classes on the Bible in public high schools.

Political parties promote competition, which can be healthy and beneficial for democracy. Competition can create incentives for parties to appeal to the common good in an attempt to obtain more members and votes. Healthy competition can also generate new ideas and promote innovation that benefits the public. Competition can also promote the adoption of policies that originated from opposition parties when those policies serve the greater good.

Another critical role of parties is to allow voters to hold the government accountable. If voters are unhappy with the controlling party, they can vote for members of the other party in the next election. This keeps the government responsive to the people, which is a touchstone of representative democracy. Didi Kuo, a democracy scholar at Stanford University, affirms that political parties are critical to a functioning democracy. "When parties perform their duties effectively, they integrate citizens into politics, keep radical candidates out of power, and negotiate between competing powerful interests,"[7] says Kuo.

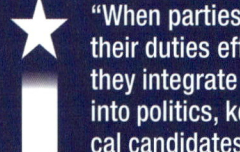

"When parties perform their duties effectively, they integrate citizens into politics, keep radical candidates out of power, and negotiate between competing powerful interests."[7]

—Didi Kuo, democracy scholar at Stanford University

The Democratic Party

The Democratic Party is the oldest political party in the United States. However, it has significantly changed since it was established over two hundred years ago. During the 1800s the Democratic Party supported slavery and opposed civil rights reforms after the American Civil War in an effort to keep the support of southerners. By the mid-1900s the Democratic Party had shifted ideologically into a party that supported organized labor and civil rights reform. Since President Franklin D. Roosevelt's New Deal in the 1930s—which was a response to help end the Great Depression and rebuild the US economy—the Democratic Party has also supported greater government intervention in the economy.

Members of the Democratic Party are Democrats. Democrats are aligned with liberal or progressive ideologies. Democrats tend to believe in a strong government that intervenes in the economy and provides social services to promote equality and enhance the health, safety, and well-being of individuals. They also tend to believe that the government should not interfere in people's private or social lives. Democrats tend to support the rights of minorities, LGBTQ people, and women. They also tend to support abortion rights and gun control measures.

The Republican Party

The Republican Party is the other major political party in the United States. During the 1800s the Republican Party opposed extending slavery to new territories in the United States and ultimately advocated for the end of slavery. During the 1900s and 2000s, the Republican Party supported low taxes, conservative social policies, and laissez-faire capitalism, which means little to no government intervention in the economy.

Members of the Republican Party are known as Republicans. Republicans are aligned with conservative or traditional ideologies. Republicans believe in a smaller federal government and thus support control by state and local governments. They tend to oppose abortion rights and gun control measures. Recently, they have been anti-immigration.

Demographic Characteristics of Both Parties

Because the two major parties are guided by different ideologies, they appeal to different types of voters. For example, as a group, those who vote for Democratic candidates are more racially diverse than those who vote for Republican candidates. Likewise, younger voters are more likely to vote Democrat than older voters.

The race and ethnicity, education, gender, age, and religious affiliation of voters are associated with different party affiliations. According to a 2020 Pew Research Center report, the Republican Party attracts more White men without a college degree, residents of rural communities in the South, and people who often attend religious services than does the Democratic Party. By contrast, the Democratic Party attracts more Black women, residents of urban communities in the Northeast, and people without a religious affiliation than does the Republican Party. The same report shows that 40 percent of registered Democrats are Black, Hispanic, Asian, and other non-White racial groups, whereas only 17 percent of registered Republicans are non-White. In terms of education, more college-educated people are affiliated with the Democratic Party. Millennials—people aged twenty-four to thirty-nine in 2020—favor the Democratic Party more than older voters do: 54 percent of Millennials identify with the Democratic Party or lean Democrat, while 38 percent identify with the Republican Party or lean Republican. Women are more likely than men to be affiliated with the Democratic Party. In terms of religion, the Republican Party has a higher percentage of Christian members than does the Democratic Party.

The demographic makeup of the United States is changing, but no one knows for sure how those changes will affect party affiliation. Many political scientists believe that the shifting demo-

The demographic makeup of the United States is changing, with the population becoming more racially and ethnically diverse. Political commentators disagree on how this will affect the two major political parties.

graphic trends will favor the Democratic Party, particularly as the country becomes more racially diverse. However, some experts believe that the increasing diversity will not help Democrats as much as some expect. In reviewing increased racial diversity, *New York Times* election correspondent Nate Cohn explains, "One reason demographic change has failed to transform electoral politics is that the increased diversity of the electorate has come not mainly from Black voters but from Hispanic, Asian-American and multiracial voters. Those groups back Democrats, but not always by overwhelmingly large margins."[8]

Political parties have played a vital role in US politics since the nation was founded. The two major political parties have organized the political process for voters, candidates, and elected officials. Although the ideologies of the Democratic and Republican parties have shifted over time, their influence over American politics has not. Going forward, demographic trends may impact the parties' membership and may prompt shifts in policy positions as both parties compete for power.

CHAPTER TWO

Political Parties and Elections

Bernie Sanders, a US senator from Vermont, has twice run for president. And although he is officially an independent, both times—in 2016 and again in 2020—he sought the Democratic Party nomination for president. Many political commentators were shocked that he chose to run as a Democrat after a successful political career as an independent. When asked why he was running as a Democrat in 2016, Sanders explained that it is difficult to attract attention from the news media as an independent. "In terms of media coverage," he said, "you had to run within the Democratic Party."[9] He also cited the difficulty of raising money as an independent.

Consumer advocate Ralph Nader, who ran for president as a third-party and independent candidate in four elections in the 1990s and early 2000s, cites another difficulty for candidates who are not affiliated with either of the two major political parties. They face many obstacles in terms of getting their names on ballots. "Just appearing on the ballot is a challenge for independent candidates,"[10] he says. Nader is referring to laws that impose requirements on independent and third-party candidates seeking a spot on the ballot. Those laws, as well as most election and voting laws, are primarily controlled by state and local governments. For example, state laws generally dictate when primary elections are held and who can vote by mail.

Nevertheless, the two major political parties exert a lot of control over some key aspects of elections. Candidates who are affiliated with a major party have advantages over nonaffiliated candidates, including easier access to the ballot and money for campaigning. Furthermore, given the major parties' stake in the outcomes of elections, the Democratic and Republican parties are active in shaping election and voting laws. Because most elected officials at state and local levels belong to one of the major parties, the two parties exert a strong influence over elections.

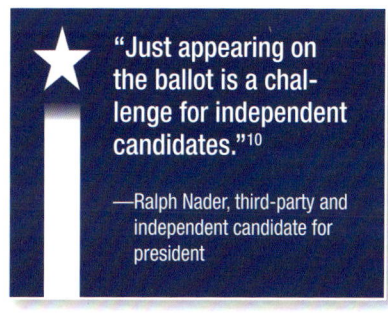

"Just appearing on the ballot is a challenge for independent candidates."[10]

—Ralph Nader, third-party and independent candidate for president

Ballot Access

State laws regulate whether a political party has the right to list its candidate on an election ballot. These laws are known as ballot access laws. Generally, only parties that have demonstrated enough support from voters—usually based on votes earned in a

Senator Bernie Sanders, an independent from Vermont, addresses supporters during a 2020 presidential campaign rally. He has cited the difficulty of attracting media attention as one reason he ran as a Democrat rather than as an independent.

prior election or the collection of supporters' signatures—can access the ballots. Generally, the Republican and Democratic parties have automatic access to the ballots. In other words, Republican and Democratic candidates can appear on ballots without having to demonstrate voter support. If more than one Republican or Democrat wants to run for a particular office, the party uses a process to select one nominee. For example, although the process of becoming a major-party nominee for president is arduous, once the nominee has been selected, adding the nominee's name to the ballot is easy.

Unlike Democrats and Republicans, third-party and independent candidates must fight their way onto the ballot. Depending on a state's law, a third-party candidate may have to collect a large number of signatures from registered voters to qualify for the ballot. Independent candidates often face similar requirements to make it to the ballot. For example, in Florida an independent candidate for president had to collect signatures from 132,781 registered voters to appear on the 2020 general election ballot. In Texas that candidate needed signatures from 89,693 registered voters who did not vote in either major party's presidential primary.

It is particularly difficult for a third-party or independent presidential candidate to make it onto the general election ballot in all states. In 1996, 2000, 2004, and 2008, Nader ran for president as a third-party and independent candidate. Although he attempted to fulfill the requirements to appear on all state ballots, he fell short in all elections. In a 2004 interview, Nader called the signature requirements unfair. "There's a tremendous bias in state laws against third parties and independent candidates bred by the two major parties, who pass these laws."[11] Nader also claimed that members of the major parties had worked to keep him off the ballot in many states. Nader's campaigns highlight a huge hurdle that non-major-party candidates face when running for elective office.

Voter Turnout Ads on Social Media

In the 2020 election, political parties spent a lot of money to encourage people to vote—and a significant chunk of that money went toward ads on social media. The Republican Party, for instance, spent $60 million on a digital get-out-the-vote campaign. This represented a stark increase from the $3 million it spent on similar efforts in 2016. A lot of that money went toward ads on Facebook.

Democratic presidential nominee Joe Biden also spent a lot of money on voter turnout ads on Facebook—more, in fact, than did presidential nominee Donald Trump, according to an article in *MIT Technology Review*. Most of Biden's voter turnout ads appeared earlier in the campaign cycle, given the Democrats' focus on mail-in and early voting due to the pandemic. However, Trump spent more on voter turnout ads on Facebook in the final weeks before the election.

The direct impact of such ads on voter turnout cannot be traced. "But what is clear is that historic turnout bolstered Republican and Democratic performance in the 2020 election, and that mail-in and early voting skewed heavily toward Democrats while same-day voting favored Republicans," Tate Ryan-Mosley explained in the *MIT Technology Review* article.

Tate Ryan-Mosley, "Republicans Spent Millions on Last-Minute Voting Ads on Facebook," *MIT Technology Review*, November 9, 2020. www.technologyreview.com.

Campaign Finances

A challenge that almost every candidate for elective office faces is raising money. That is because running for elective office is expensive. This is true for national offices as well as state and local offices. Estimates indicate that $6.6 billion was spent on the 2020 presidential election, which is considered the most expensive election in US history. In 2021 the major-party candidates for governor of Virginia raised a combined total of $115 million, of which almost $60 million was spent on political ads, according to the nonpartisan nonprofit Virginia Public Access Project.

To reach potential voters, candidates must get their names and message out. Candidates campaign in person, traveling throughout the area they hope to represent. A presidential candidate campaigns across the United States, whereas a candidate running for governor campaigns across a state. As a result,

During a 2018 campaign stop, Georgia gubernatorial candidate Stacey Abrams urges her supporters to vote. Candidates for public office spend a lot of time and money on travel and advertising, and political parties often help with fund-raising and organization.

candidates incur travel expenses for themselves and their campaign staff, which add up quickly. As they travel, they may hold rallies, visit popular local businesses, and meet with residents in small groups. In addition to in-person campaigning, candidates run media campaigns, which may involve television, radio, and social media advertisements. They may send letters and brochures to potential voters to promote themselves. All of these campaign activities cost money.

The two major parties are organized to assist with campaign finances. They have access to donors and a system for distributing donations to their candidates. Although state and federal laws govern campaign financing, the Democratic and Republican parties are well equipped to navigate these complicated laws. Third parties, however, lack a large membership from which they can seek donations. They also tend to be less organized from an administrative level, which hampers their ability to raise money and coordinate fund-raising efforts.

As a result, candidates running as Democrats and Republicans generally have better-funded campaigns. More money means a bigger advertising budget, more travel, and larger rallies—all of which allow major-party candidates to get their names and messages out to a larger audience. Third-party and independent candidates tend to have less money to support a wide-reaching campaign, which limits their ability to connect with potential voters.

Candidates can raise money to pay for their campaigns from individuals, party committees, and political action committees (PACs). PACs are organizations that raise and spend money to support or oppose political candidates. They may also spend money to support or oppose specific legislation or ballot initiatives. Some PACs are established by corporations, labor unions, or other organizations. PACs that are not associated with an organization are funded by members of the general public. PACs can donate directly to a candidate's campaign, but they are limited in how much they can receive from individual donors and how much they can give to candidates. For example, PACs may contribute up to $5,000 per year to a candidate in each election.

Super PACs have been created as a workaround to the contribution limits of PACs, and they spend a lot of money to affect election outcomes. Super PACs, which have no limits on how much they can collect from individual donors and corporations, cannot donate directly to candidates. Instead, super PACs can pay for independently produced ads and other materials that support or attack specific candidates. According to Thomas E. Mann and Anthony Corrado, senior fellows at the Brookings Institution, most super PACs are created to support a certain candidate of either of the two major parties. Many are run "by former party officials or operatives with long histories within and strong links to their parties,"[12] Mann and Corrado explain. The ultimate impact of super PACs on third-party candidates is unclear, because they are a relatively new creation. However, 2004 Green Party presidential nominee David

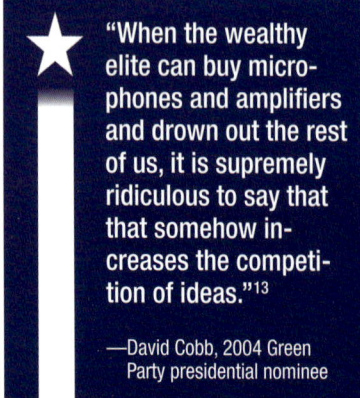

"When the wealthy elite can buy microphones and amplifiers and drown out the rest of us, it is supremely ridiculous to say that that somehow increases the competition of ideas."[13]

—David Cobb, 2004 Green Party presidential nominee

Cobb believes super PACs "are squashing competition." The lack of limits on fundraising and spending means that some super PACs have a lot of money, much of which is collected from wealthy individuals. "When the wealthy elite can buy microphones and amplifiers and drown out the rest of us, it is supremely ridiculous to say that that somehow increases the competition of ideas,"[13] says Cobb.

Controlling the Voting Process

In addition to campaigns, political parties get involved with voting laws, which control the voting process. Voting laws, for the most part, are set by state and local governments. However, political parties impact voting laws in several ways. For example, state legislators can amend voting laws in a way that benefits their party. This has been happening a lot recently, with Republican lawmakers pushing for more restrictive voting laws and Democratic lawmakers pushing for laws that make it easier to vote. Lawmakers in both parties see these changes as either harmful or beneficial to their party's candidates—and elections in general.

Many of the recent changes in election laws have come about in response to the 2020 election. Given the complications of getting voters to the polls on Election Day during the pandemic, many states changed their rules to allow increased mail-in ballots (or absentee ballots) and early voting in 2020. An unprecedented number of people—almost 70 percent of voters, as estimated by the US Census Bureau—voted by mail or voted before Election Day in the 2020 general election.

State Voting Laws

Before the votes were even tallied, Trump alleged fraud in terms of who voted and how votes were being counted. Although no evidence of fraud has been found, Republican lawmakers around the country have responded by tightening voting laws in their states. Some of these laws, such as laws targeting college students who do not live where they are registered to vote, make it harder to vote absentee. Other laws, known as voter ID laws, require that specific forms of identification be shown at the polls to prove a voter's identity. For example, strict voter ID laws may require that voters present a state-issued photo ID, such as a driver's license, at the polls. The Brennan Center for Justice says that some eligible voters, as many as 11 percent, do not have the type of IDs required by strict voter ID laws.

Democratic lawmakers have responded to these efforts by enacting laws that make it easier to vote in their states. Types of expansive voting laws include making it easier to vote by mail, such as by allowing any voter to vote absentee without needing to provide an excuse for not being able to vote in person on Election Day. Other expansive voting laws restore voting rights to people with a felony conviction, who are not allowed to vote in some states.

Georgia election workers sort ballots during a recount stemming from the November 2020 presidential election. Although recounts such as this one found no evidence of fraud, many states have passed new voting laws.

Other bills and laws target the vote-counting process. CNN analyst Harry Enten categorizes the proposed voting bills across the country into two types: those that change how people vote and those that change how votes are counted. "The former has received much of the attention from Democrats trying to counter Republicans, but it is the latter that is by far a clearer threat to democracy," he says. Enten explains that laws that make it harder to vote do not deter most voters; many simply find another way to vote, even if it is inconvenient. However, once their votes are cast, voters hope that their votes will be counted but "can do very little, if they aren't,"[14] says Enten.

Attempts to change how votes are counted are a direct response to Trump's unsupported allegations of fraud. He demanded that election officials in key states recount the votes. Recounts were conducted in these states—in some cases more than once—but no evidence of fraud was found in the vote-counting process. Despite this, many of these proposed laws decrease the proof required to trigger a vote recount or to prove that a voter engaged in fraud. Others impose criminal penalties if an election official makes a mistake.

A Federal Voting Rights Bill

In addition to their efforts to expand voting laws in various states, Democrats have also been trying to pass a federal voting rights bill in Congress. The Freedom to Vote: John R. Lewis Act—named after the long-serving US representative from Georgia who fought for civil rights and died in 2020—seeks to standardize voting election laws across the United States. Republican lawmakers support continued state control over voting. President Joe Biden, a Democrat, favors standardized voting laws for the nation as a whole, saying it would "restore and expand voting protections and prevent voter suppression."[15] As of April 2022, Congress had not passed a new voting rights bill. However, the competing efforts of both parties indicate that the battle over voting laws is far from over.

From Party Bosses to Primaries

Until the late 1960s, political parties had more control over their nominees, particularly presidential nominees. Political party bosses carefully vetted and selected candidates for the country's highest office, as well as other offices. They evaluated potential candidates and excluded those who had a questionable past or were otherwise poor choices. The role of party bosses changed with the modern presidential primary system, which Walter Shapiro of the Brennan Center for Justice says emerged after the 1968 election.

Now the presidential nomination process involves a primary election, in which potential candidates face off in a series of primaries and caucuses. The primary election is a preliminary election that determines which candidates will run for president for each party. The rules for primaries vary by state, but generally, the winner of a state's primary earns votes from party delegates, who formally cast their votes at their party's national convention. The candidate who earns the most votes is officially nominated as the party's candidate.

Although political parties still serve an important role in the nomination process, their role has changed. According to Shapiro, the power to nominate candidates has "shifted from political bosses to partisan voters."

Walter Shapiro, "Rationalizing the Presidential Nomination Process," Brennan Center for Justice, October 28, 2021. www.brennancenter.org.

Given that the two major parties battle for power via elections, they exert influence over the election process when they can, such as by shaping important voting laws. Candidates also receive benefits from being affiliated with one of the two major parties, such as easier access to the ballot and campaign money. As a result, elections reinforce the two-party system in the United States.

CHAPTER THREE

Gerrymandering to Create Election Advantage

In 2019 the US Supreme Court considered challenges to the maps of congressional districts in North Carolina and Maryland. The plaintiffs who brought the cases alleged that the maps discriminated against members of their political party. The plaintiffs in the North Carolina case argued that the new congressional district maps discriminated against Democrats, while the Maryland plaintiffs argued that the maps discriminated against Republicans. At the heart of the case was the issue of gerrymandering, which is the drawing of congressional district maps for the benefit of a political party.

The Supreme Court found that the North Carolina and Maryland maps were highly partisan, meaning that they advantaged one party more than the other. In North Carolina, Republican legislators led the redistricting effort. They instructed their mapmaker to draw a map such that ten Republicans and three Democrats would win their state's seats in the US House of Representatives. One of the two Republicans chairing the redistricting committee said, "I think electing Republicans is better than electing Democrats. So I drew this map to help foster what I think is better for the country."[16] In Maryland the Democratic governor led the redistricting effort. The governor said he intended to "use the redistricting process to change the overall composition of Maryland's congressional delegation to 7 Democrats and 1 Republican by flipping"[17] one district. To flip that district, 360,000 voters were strategically moved out of the district and 350,000 voters were moved into the district. The result was to increase the number of Democratic voters by the amount needed to win the district. In the elections following redistricting, the new maps in both states produced the results that were anticipated.

The court found that the new maps in both states were overly partisan but left the maps in place. The reason given (in the majority opinion) is that federal courts do not have the power to interfere with partisan redistricting. The author of that opinion, Chief Justice John Roberts, noted that partisan gerrymandering can produce unjust results. "Excessive partisanship in districting leads to results that reasonably seem unjust," Roberts wrote. However, the court concluded that the issue of gerrymandering is a political question appropriate for Congress to resolve, not the responsibility of federal courts. Roberts stated that federal judges

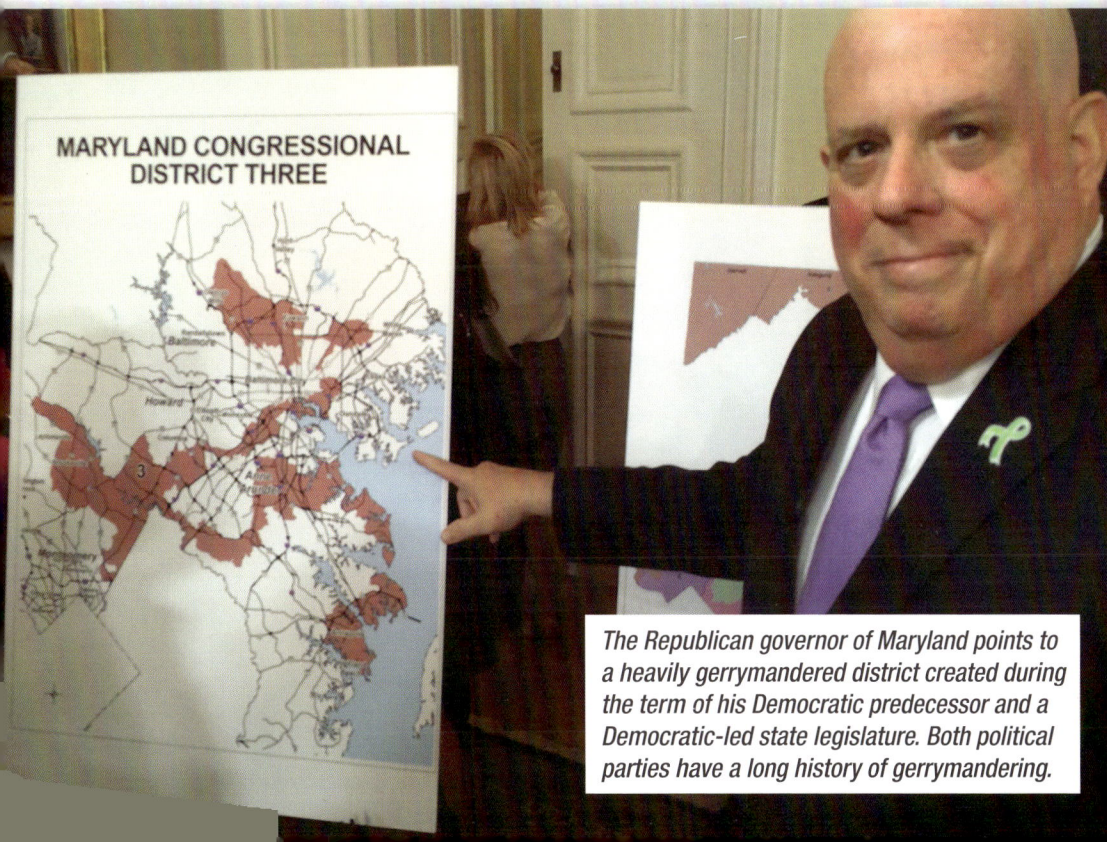

The Republican governor of Maryland points to a heavily gerrymandered district created during the term of his Democratic predecessor and a Democratic-led state legislature. Both political parties have a long history of gerrymandering.

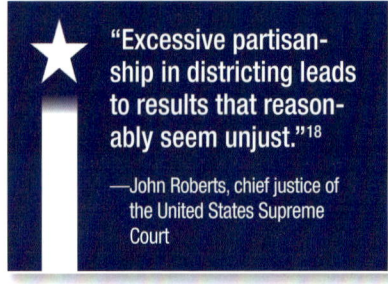

"Excessive partisanship in districting leads to results that reasonably seem unjust."[18]

—John Roberts, chief justice of the United States Supreme Court

have no authority "to reallocate political power between the two major political parties."[18]

Emboldened by that decision, both parties have continued their efforts—either to gerrymander or fight against it. In Ohio in 2021, for instance, Democrats challenged the legislative districts drawn by Republicans, who controlled the state government. A lawsuit filed by Democrats claimed that the state's newly drawn congressional map gave Republicans an unfair advantage. The Supreme Court of the State of Ohio agreed and struck down Ohio's gerrymandered map, finding that it violated the state constitution. The court said that the new map drawn by Republicans would ensure that Republicans would win more congressional seats than the party normally wins in terms of the popular vote. "When the dealer stacks the deck in advance," the court's ruling stated, "the house usually wins. That perhaps explains how a party that generally musters no more than 55 percent of the statewide popular vote is positioned to reliably win anywhere from 75 percent to 80 percent of the seats in the Ohio congressional delegation." The court found that the "skewed result just does not add up," and ordered the state to draw a new map without "partisan considerations."[19]

When Redistricting Becomes Gerrymandering

Court challenges to district maps are brought after new maps are drawn in a process known as redistricting, which happens every ten years. Redistricting is the process of redrawing the maps outlining state legislative and US congressional districts based on the most recent US Census data. Districts are geographic areas from which members of the US House of Representatives and state legislatures are elected. (City councils, county commissions, and school boards are often also divided into districts.) District boundaries are redrawn to account for population changes. Ideally, each

Redistricting Commissions

One way to prevent gerrymandering is to shift the redistricting responsibility from state legislatures to nonlegislative commissions. Such commissions are not affiliated with a political party, suggesting that these commissions will draw fairer maps. According to the National Conference of State Legislatures, as of December 2021, ten states had a commission or board that is primarily responsible for drawing congressional districts. Experts say that the design of the commission—including how commissioners are selected and how the maps are approved—impacts whether the redistricting process is actually independent and free of partisan pressure.

In California the Citizens Redistricting Commission is composed of fourteen commissioners who are registered voters. Applicants apply to serve on the commission, and government auditors select sixty applicants. Legislative leaders can reduce that pool, from which government auditors select eight using a lottery. The eight selected commissioners then choose six additional commissioners. The makeup of the commission must be five Democrats, five Republicans, and four individuals not affiliated with either party. Three Democratic commissioners, three Republican commissioners, and three commissioners without party affiliation must approve any new district boundaries.

elected official represents roughly the same number of people, which complies with the principle of one person, one vote.

Gerrymandering creates district maps that advantage one political party. District maps that have been gerrymandered sometimes have odd shapes or strange boundaries, such as right through the middle of a neighborhood. However, not all gerrymandered maps are oddly shaped. The goal of the party drawing the map is to maintain or increase its political power by optimizing its candidates' chances of getting elected. For example, if Democrats were engaged in gerrymandering, they would draw district maps to give Democrats a better chance of winning more seats in Congress. Although there is no way of knowing how voters will ultimately vote, the parties consider voting history as well as party affiliation of the registered voters.

There are two main ways to configure the maps to benefit a party. One is known as packing. Packing a district means drawing the map to include as many of the opposing party's voters as possible. Although the voters in the packed district can likely elect their preferred candidate, their party's strength is diluted in surrounding districts. As a result, the party that controlled redistricting has a better chance of winning the surrounding districts. For example, if Republicans draw a map to pack one district with likely Democratic voters, they will probably lose that district but win the surrounding ones.

By contrast, "cracking" divides clusters of opposition voters among several districts to ensure that the opposition voters will be outnumbered in each district. For example, if Democrats draw a map to spread likely Republican voters into several districts, they dilute the power of the Republican voters. As a result, Democrats would have a better chance of winning those districts.

Who Gerrymanders?

The US Constitution does not specify the actual process that states must follow when drawing congressional maps. As a result, the states are left to design their own procedures for creating the maps, and the states vary in the way they redistrict. In most states, new district maps are drawn by the state legislature, subject to veto by the governor. In those states, when one political party controls both houses of a state legislature and the governor's office, that party can generally draw the maps in a way that benefits the party. However, when the legislature and the governor are from different parties, it is less likely that gerrymandering will occur. Other states exclude the governor from redistricting, leaving the process entirely in the hands of the legislature.

Some states have different processes for redistricting, such as delegating it to a commission. Generally, states that use commissions have done so to reduce concerns that one-party-dominated legislatures will gerrymander. Some redistricting commissions are advisory bodies that make recommendations to the legislature, with the legislature ultimately deciding whether to accept the recommended boundaries. Others are independent commissions

New Yorkers consider possible district maps during a redistricting advisory commission meeting. Some states have independent or advisory commissions while others leave redistricting to legislators.

that have the power to determine the boundaries. The commissions also vary in terms of their independence from party influence. Some require that the commissions be nonpartisan, meaning that many members are not affiliated with any major party. Others are bipartisan, meaning that there are an equal number of Democrats and Republicans on the commission. Those who support independent commissions generally believe that they can prevent partisan gerrymandering.

The fact is that both Republicans and Democrats gerrymander when they can. According to Stephen Ohlemacher, an editor for the Associated Press, "Gerrymandering has a long history in the United States, pursued enthusiastically by both Democrats and Republicans."[20] After the 2010 elections, the Republican Party controlled most state legislatures, when redistricting occurred after the 2010 census. According to Justin Levitt, a law professor and redistricting expert at Loyola Law School in

> "Gerrymandering has a long history in the United States, pursued enthusiastically by both Democrats and Republicans."[20]
>
> —Stephen Ohlemacher, editor for the Associated Press

Los Angeles, Republicans controlled the redistricting process for 210 House districts, whereas Democrats controlled it for only 44 districts in that cycle. As a result, Republicans were able to draw the maps to their advantage in many states, making the 2010 redistricting cycle advantageous for the Republican Party. Despite Republican candidates receiving 1.4 million fewer votes overall than their Democratic opponents, in 2012 the Republicans held thirty-three more seats in the House of Representatives. In the 2010 redistricting cycle, Democrats did the same thing in states where they had control.

As of 2022, Republicans controlled more state governments than did Democrats, providing an advantage to Republicans in terms of redistricting in this latest cycle. Republicans are trying to pick up seats in several key states, including North Carolina and Georgia. Democrats have fewer options for gaining seats and are focusing on states they control, such as New York. This may explain why Democrats are fighting to stop gerrymandering, such as by seeking to prohibit it with federal legislation and challenging particular maps through litigation in state courts.

How Gerrymandering Hurts Democracy

Although population changes necessitate redistricting, drawing maps to benefit a particular party is bad for democracy. Representative democracy is supposed to be a system in which elected officials represent the people, who have the power to vote elected officials out of office if they are not doing their job well. However, some experts characterize the redistricting process in many states as allowing politicians to choose which voters they represent. "Rather than voters choosing their representatives, gerrymandering empowers politicians to choose their voters,"[21] explain democracy scholars Julia Kirschenbaum and Michael Li of the Brennan Center for Justice.

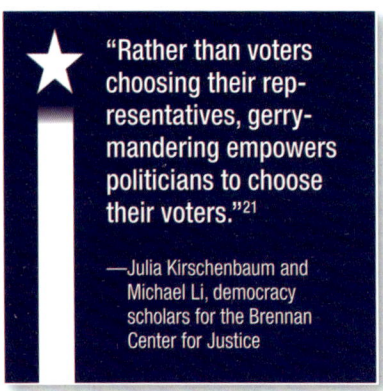

"Rather than voters choosing their representatives, gerrymandering empowers politicians to choose their voters."[21]

—Julia Kirschenbaum and Michael Li, democracy scholars for the Brennan Center for Justice

Protesters gather outside the US Supreme Court in 2017 as the justices hear arguments in a partisan gerrymandering case. Gerrymandering attempts to give one party an advantage over the other.

Gerrymandering is designed to impact election outcomes by giving one party a strong advantage over the other. Although voters still have the right to vote in gerrymandered districts, voters may feel like their vote does not matter. Voters who have been moved, via map drawing, to districts where their party has little chance of winning may believe their vote counts less than other votes. They may also feel their opinion about how government should work is unimportant. Former president Barack Obama described the process of gerrymandering as "trying to tilt the playing field." When accusing Republicans of gerrymandering in 2021, Obama said, "Their plan is to control state legislatures and congressional delegations before a single vote is cast," which "is not how democracy is supposed to work."[22]

Communities of Color

Gerrymandering disproportionately affects communities of color. This mainly stems from the fact that race is a strong predictor of party affiliation. For instance, voters of color vote predominately

Technology's Impact on Gerrymandering

Advances in technology are making gerrymandering easier and worse. With computer algorithms and increased data about voters, map drawers can gerrymander with more precision than ever. According to journalist Vann R. Newkirk II, the political mapmaking business is worth millions of dollars and involves consultants, lawyers, voting data, specialized software, and even supercomputers.

In the past, the map-drawing process was done in pencil on paper. John Ryder, who was the former general counsel of the Republican National Committee, started working on redistricting in the 1970s. "When I started doing this in the mid-70s, we were using handheld calculators, paper maps, pencils, and really big erasers. It was pretty primitive," he says. Since then, computer software programs have been developed to analyze large quantities of US Census data as well as other voter data. So-called big data—large and complex data sets—have transformed the way that maps are drawn. By analyzing multiple kinds of data, the parties believe they can accurately predict how voters will vote in the future, which affects how the maps are drawn.

Quoted in Vann R. Newkirk II, "How Redistricting Became a Technological Arms Race," *The Atlantic*, October 28, 2017. www.theatlantic.com.

---

for Democrats. As a result, when drawing maps to advantage a party, district boundaries are often moved to dilute or amplify the power of voters of color. According to Samuel Wang, director of the Princeton Gerrymandering Project, a minority community can be divided between districts, making them a small percentage of the electorate with little political power. This is known as cracking. Alternatively, a minority community can be crammed into a single district so that the community's influence is reduced in other districts, which is known as packing. Whatever technique is used, the goal is to benefit the party in charge of drawing the maps.

Historical residential factors make it easy to target communities of color when drawing maps. For example, people have historically congregated in neighborhoods with people of the same race. As Kirschenbaum and Li explain, "Because of residential segregation, it is much easier for map drawers to pack or crack communities of color to achieve maximum political advantage."[23]

Reducing the political power of communities of color means that the interests of those groups may be less protected. That is because elected representatives have fewer incentives to respond to the communities' needs and concerns if the communities' votes will not keep them in or push them out of office. In other words, if communities of color, such as Black and Latino communities, are denied political power through gerrymandering, their interests are less likely to be considered by elected officials.

Polarization

Some experts believe that in addition to harming communities of color, gerrymandering has contributed to increased political polarization—the divide between people based on political party identities. They believe that politicians in gerrymandered districts become more extreme because their elections are less competitive. This in turn gives politicians little incentive to appeal to moderate voters. Moderate voters, who stand at the center of the political spectrum, usually reject extreme views on either end of the ideological spectrum. When moderate voters' influence is reduced, the effect is increased polarization because elected officials will cater to their more extreme base of supporters.

However, other experts believe that gerrymandering does not increase polarization. They believe that in many areas, competitive congressional districts would be difficult to achieve even if neither party engaged in gerrymandering. That is because people have sorted themselves by political affiliation, moving to communities with people who share similar political beliefs and essentially creating areas that overwhelmingly favor one party over the other.

Partisan gerrymandering is not new. However, due to the growing division between the parties, gerrymandering has become a hot issue. Unless there is a significant change in federal law or the processes by which states redistrict, Democrats and Republicans are likely to gerrymander when they can, prompting legal challenges in courts across the nation.

CHAPTER FOUR

Hyperpartisanship Threatens Democracy

On January 6, 2021, Congress met at the US Capitol to certify the results of the 2020 presidential election, which was one of the most partisan elections in US history. Two miles (3.2 km) away, outgoing president Donald Trump spoke to a group of his supporters, alleging that the election was stolen. He urged his supporters to march on the Capitol to demand that Congress not certify the election results. After the speech ended, a mob of Trump supporters, some of whom were armed, proceeded to the Capitol and stormed the building to stop the election certification. The rioters outnumbered US Capitol Police officers, which allowed them to breach the Capitol. Rioters broke windows and vandalized the offices of Congress members. Some even expressed violent intentions toward members of Congress and then–vice president Mike Pence for refusing to overturn the election in Trump's favor. Several people died, and many were injured in connection with the attack.

    The January 6 attack is an example of what happens when partisanship goes too far. Historically, most losers of elections acknowledge the loss and congratulate the winner even when they feel great disappointment at the outcome. In this case, the loser contended that he had won. In challenging the validity of the election, without any evidence to support his allegations, Trump was challenging a cornerstone of democracy. Without evidence that votes were cast or counted unfairly or illegally, Trump sought to foster distrust in America's elections. And he emboldened some of his supporters to join his efforts. The January 6 attack could have brought Democrats and Republicans together in defense of democracy. Instead, many Republican lawmakers rallied around a false narrative, further widening the gap between the two parties and their supporters and heightening the extreme level of partisanship that threatens the functioning of government.

The Other Party Is Cast as the Enemy

Given the partisan divide between Americans, the stakes of recent elections have been higher than ever. Surveys conducted shortly before the 2020 election found unusually high levels of stress, fear, and anxiety among voters. "People believe that the outcome of this election is going to have a serious effect on their lives, and I

Rioters clash with police as at they try to force their way into the Capitol building on January 6, 2021. The January 6 attack is an example of what happens when partisanship goes too far.

think beyond that, on their safety,"[24] said Afton Kapuscinski, director of the Psychological Services Center at Syracuse University.

In the run-up to that election, both political parties claimed that the nation's future was at stake—and both painted dire though considerably different pictures of that future. The differences in the futures feared by Republicans and Democrats are mainly due to the way Americans have aligned political parties with their identity. When politics are integral to identity, elections and politics become personal. In other words, the parties no longer represent just different ideologies; they represent different ways of life. In fact, parents from both parties (35 percent of Republicans and 45 percent of Democrats) have said they do not want their children to marry people affiliated with the other party, according to a 2019 report by the Public Religion Research Institute.

Many Americans support a political party not because of its bold and visionary ideas but because they dislike and distrust the other party. And these feelings are growing. In a 2016 Pew

Distrust in Government

Americans distrust the federal government's ability to solve problems. According to a 2021 survey conducted on behalf of Grinnell College, only 7 percent of Americans have a high level of trust in the federal government to propose good solutions to problems within their communities. "Trust in political institutions is the glue that holds democracies together and allows them to weather crises over time," says Danielle Lussier, a professor of political science at Grinnell College. "While there will always be some skepticism toward the government, when a majority of people express distrust in elected officials, the legitimacy of the constitutional order is called into question."

Distrust in government has consequences, especially when distrust is combined with hyperpartisanship. When people do not trust the government, it makes it harder for the government to conduct its regular business. Also the public becomes more resistant to the government, which means that people may not cooperate with government agencies. For example, a study published in the *Lancet* examined trust in government in 177 countries and found that higher levels of trust in government were significantly associated with fewer COVID-19 infections.

Quoted in Grinnell College, "52% of Americans Believe Democracy Facing 'Major Threat,'" October 20, 2021. www.grinnell.edu.

Research Center poll, many Americans (55 percent of Democrats and 49 percent of Republicans) said they fear the other party. A 2019 study by political scientists at Louisiana State University and the University of Maryland found an even more concerning level of distrust between members of the two parties. According to that study, more than 42 percent of both Democrats and Republicans view the other party as "downright evil."[25] Each side sees the other as a threat—an enemy to be defeated.

In this environment, public policy disagreements and debate—which are a normal and even desirable aspect of a healthy democracy—devolve into extreme partisanship and negativity. When elected officials and members of the general public vilify people who hold different views, debate and discussion become impossible. Instead of functioning as "institutions that help us coordinate candidates, policies, and voters," political parties "become institutions that reinforce negative projections"[26] and disrupt the ability to govern, notes political science professor Jennifer Victor.

Stalled Legislation

Joe Biden, who has frequently acknowledged the division and animosity, has pleaded with Americans to set aside partisan differences for the good of the country. During his presidential campaign, he stood where Abraham Lincoln gave the Gettysburg Address and echoed similar sentiments. "Today, once again, we are a house divided." Biden blamed extreme partisanship for fueling division and distrust between Americans. He continued, "Hope is elusive. Too many Americans see our public life not as an arena for mediation of our differences. Rather, they see it as an occasion for total, unrelenting partisan warfare. Instead of treating the other party as the opposition, we treat them as the enemy. This must end."[27]

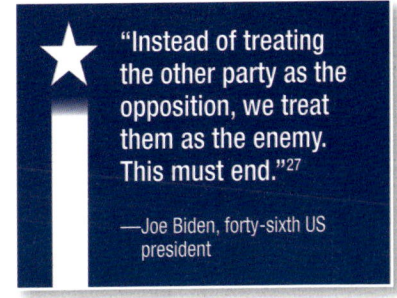

"Instead of treating the other party as the opposition, we treat them as the enemy. This must end."[27]

—Joe Biden, forty-sixth US president

However, partisan warfare did not end when Biden was sworn in as president. During that first year, hyperpartisanship

Pittsburgh's Fern Hollow Bridge (pictured) collapsed in January 2022, just hours before President Biden's planned visit. Biden was coming there to talk about his new infrastructure law, which had been delayed for months despite bipartisan support.

plagued Congress—even stalling the passage of legislation that had support from both parties. For example, in March 2021, Biden announced his initiative to rebuild the nation's economy, which included investing in infrastructure. The infrastructure portion of Biden's initiative sought money to repair roads and aging bridges all across the country. This plan would also go a long way toward revitalizing the economy after the destruction caused by the COVID-19 pandemic. Because both Republicans and Democrats supported investing in infrastructure, longtime congressional observers expected an infrastructure bill to pass fairly quickly. But that did not happen. It took over four months after Biden announced his proposed infrastructure package for the Senate to pass a bipartisan bill. In August 2021 the Senate passed a $1 trillion infrastructure bill with 69 votes, including 19 by Republicans. The bill was further delayed by another three months in the House. In November 2021 the House finally passed the infrastructure bill with 228 votes, including 13 by Republicans.

Experts have explained that the standoff was not based on a disagreement over public policy. Rather, Brookings Institution fellow Thomas E. Mann says that the months of inaction stemmed from one party's desire not to let the other party appear to win. Mann says that the goal of the Republican Party, in this case, was to "drag down Biden's approval rating and discredit the Democratic Party any way they can. Anything that can hurt them or blame them is a popular thing."[28] In other words, Congress was stalling on passing popular legislation because of extreme partisanship.

Michael W. Macy, a professor of sociology at Cornell University, has a name for this. He calls it "political paralysis." Political paralysis occurs, he says, when "the parties are more interested in preventing the other side from winning than in solving problems. We have heard politicians even feel so emboldened that they can publicly acknowledge that their goal is obstruction, not problem solving."[29] Macy blames political paralysis on heightened polarization, which is the result of extreme partisanship.

Heightened polarization poses a risk to a healthy democracy by impeding the ability to govern. For generations, American lawmakers have had shared goals but often disagreed on how to achieve some of those goals. So they negotiated and often found some sort of compromise. This process is happening less often as lawmakers resort to vilifying those with whom they disagree. By labeling them as the enemy, rather than acknowledging disagreement over shared goals, negotiation and compromise become impossible. "When division involves purity and impurity, when it devolves into a pure contest between 'us' and 'them'— then there is no bargaining, because there are no negotiable principles, just team loyalties,"[30] says political scientist Lee Drutman. Political differences become a battle between good and evil, in which neither side is willing to compromise.

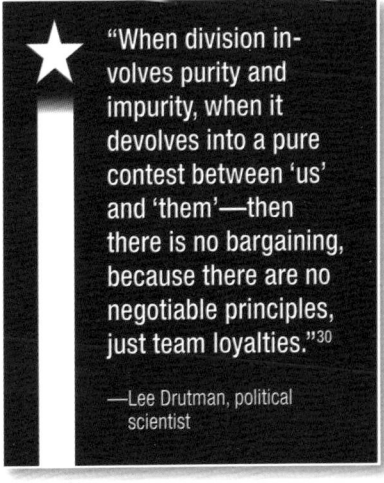

"When division involves purity and impurity, when it devolves into a pure contest between 'us' and 'them'—then there is no bargaining, because there are no negotiable principles, just team loyalties."[30]

—Lee Drutman, political scientist

Increased Power of the Executive and Judiciary

Hyperpartisanship disrupts the balance of power that was intended by the drafters of the Constitution. When the legislative branch fails to act due to hyperpartisanship, presidents increasingly use executive power to push through policy. For example, instead of trying to implement policy changes through the legislative process in Congress, a president may rely on executive orders to advance a policy agenda. In 2017, to advance his more restrictive immigration agenda, Trump issued an executive order banning travelers from seven predominately Muslim countries. More recently, Biden issued an executive order raising the minimum wage for federal contract workers to $15 an hour as part of his effort to raise the federal minimum wage. Increased use of executive power makes the presidency more powerful, which leads to higher-stakes elections. All of this fuels partisanship.

The judiciary also becomes more powerful when the legislative branch is not fulfilling its role. Drutman explains that "as hyper-partisanship has intensified legislative gridlock, more and more important decisions are left to the judiciary to resolve."[31] For example, in the 2021–2022 term, the Supreme Court was slated to address polarizing issues like abortion, guns, and religion. Congress has been unable to legislate in many of these areas due to deep division between the parties.

Drutman says that a more powerful judiciary increases the importance of who gets appointed as Supreme Court justices, which in turn leads to higher-stakes presidential elections, given that the president makes those appointments. In Congress the confirmation process for Supreme Court justice nominees has become hyperpartisan and exceedingly ugly. For example, when Justice Antonin Scalia died in February 2016, Senate majority leader Mitch McConnell, a Republican, blocked consideration of President Obama's nominee to fill the vacancy. McConnell argued that the next president should fill the seat, given that the election

Partisan Media Emphasizes Differences

There are many ways to get political news: by watching or listening to news programs on TV or radio, reading print or online newspapers, scrolling through social media, and listening to podcasts. With so many options, news providers cater to certain consumers, meaning that some target Democrats while others target Republicans. Some experts believe that watching one-sided media leads to increased partisanship, while other experts believe that it leads to mistrust in media.

In addition, the media seems to profit from divisive news, particularly when it comes to politics. Most media companies are profit-oriented businesses that compete for consumers. Outrageous and divisive news coverage attracts readers, viewers, and listeners. In other words, the media has an incentive to focus on confrontational stories. Because people are outraged when other groups threaten their identity, stories that frame one political party as attacking a core value of the other party take center stage. "As such, polarized media doesn't emphasize commonalities, it weaponizes differences; it doesn't focus on the best of the other side, it threatens you with the worst," explains journalist and author Ezra Klein.

Ezra Klein, "Why the Media Is So Polarized—and How It Polarizes Us," Vox, January 28, 2020. www.vox.com.

was *only nine months* away. But when Justice Ruth Bader Ginsburg died in September 2020, with *less than two months* to go until the next presidential election, McConnell rushed the process to ensure that President Trump's nominee would be confirmed before the election.

Challenges for Democracy

Hyperpartisanship has been identified by numerous political scientists as a challenge to democracy. Drutman predicts that the federal government may lose its ability to function, making it more difficult for the nation to meet big challenges. The pandemic is an example of a large problem that the federal government had difficulty addressing in a cohesive way. Other complex issues, like climate change, will likely require large-scale solutions that can only be feasible if enacted by the federal government. However, without an effective federal government, individual states may act on their own, resulting in piecemeal efforts across the nation.

Some scholars fear that hyperpartisanship will increase extremism. Heightened division encourages political leaders to advance more extreme views rather than searching for a middle ground. In this scenario, the most vocal and extreme partisans tend to dominate political debate, and partisan political victories take on more importance than efforts to work with people who hold different views. According to five scholars featured in a 2021 *New York Times* opinion column, voters serve as "a potential check on this cascading extremism." However, voters "must be willing to punish ideologically extreme legislators by voting them out of office. As voters have become more concerned about party labels than ideology, they have become less willing to do that, allowing cascading extremism to continue."[32]

Experts warn that hyperpartisanship will make it more difficult to meet the big challenges of the future. Climate change, which has led to massive wildfires and other extreme weather events, is one of these challenges.

Although the nation's two main political parties have always had disagreements on policy, inability to agree on basic facts is a more recent outgrowth of hyperpartisanship. Even members of the public have recognized this change. A 2018 survey conducted by the Pew Research Center found that 73 percent of Americans believe that Republicans and Democrats do not agree on basic facts. "We now live in a world where there are red facts and blue facts, and I believe these biased . . . reasoning processes fuel political conflict," says Peter Ditto, a psychology professor at the University of California, Irvine. "If someone firmly believes some fact to be true that you just as firmly believe to be false, it is hard for either of you not to see that other person as stupid, disingenuous or both."[33]

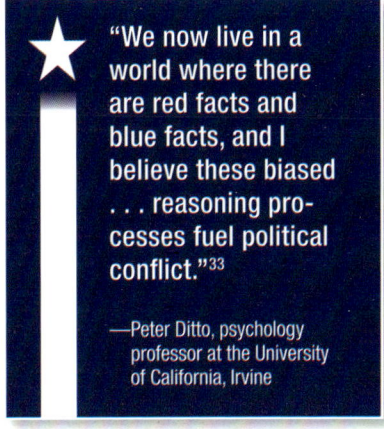

"We now live in a world where there are red facts and blue facts, and I believe these biased . . . reasoning processes fuel political conflict."[33]

—Peter Ditto, psychology professor at the University of California, Irvine

If Americans have two different visions of reality, they cannot come together to solve problems. After all, one side's version of the facts may indicate that there is no problem to solve. This leaves American democracy open to internal and external enemies, without a united citizenry to defeat them. The hyperpartisan climate in the United States is likely to continue. If Democrats and Republicans are unable to compromise on important issues, the government's ability to function will be compromised. As a result, some fear that extreme partisanship threatens US democracy.

CHAPTER FIVE

Reducing Polarization Between Parties and People

Partisan polarization is extremely high, and Democrats and Republicans are more divided than ever. They disagree about critical issues such as the economy, racial justice, and climate change. According to surveys conducted by the Pew Research Center in 2020, members of both parties believe the divisions go beyond policy issues and involve core American values. The center explains, "Republicans and Democrats agree on very little—and when they do, it often is in the shared belief that they have little in common."[34] Other data collected by the Pew Research Center found that Democrats and Republicans agree on something else: partisan divisions will continue to increase, which is problematic.

Despite the consensus that extreme partisan division is problematic, there is no clear-cut solution for reducing it. Political scientists and other scholars have been debating the issue for years. In addition to ideas that promote empathy and understanding between people, some experts suggest that changing the way elections are conducted may reduce hyperpartisanship.

Changing Primaries

One idea for reducing partisanship is to change the way primaries are conducted. In most states, the major political parties hold a primary election to determine the party's nominee for public office. How those primaries are conducted varies by state. Some states have open primaries, others have closed primaries, while some have a slightly different variation (such as partially opened or partially closed). An open primary means that any registered voter, regardless of party affiliation, can vote in the primary of either major party. A closed primary means that only voters who are affiliated with that party can vote in the party's primary. For example, Florida has closed primaries, meaning that only registered Republicans can vote in the Republican primary and only registered Democrats can vote in the Democratic primary. Florida voters who are affiliated with neither party cannot vote in either party's primary.

Those who support closed primaries believe that they protect a party's freedom of association by limiting the party's nomination process to its members. They also fear that open primaries would allow voters from the opposition party to vote for the candidate with the least chance of winning the general election, in an attempt

"Republicans and Democrats agree on very little—and when they do, it often is in the shared belief that they have little in common."[34]

—Pew Research Center, nonpartisan research organization

Voters in Missouri mark their ballots in the 2020 presidential primary. One idea for reducing partisanship is to change the way primaries are conducted.

to advantage the voters' party. However, critics of closed primaries argue that they increase polarization and extremism because the candidates have an incentive to appeal to the party's base over moderate voters. In other words, closed primaries may produce candidates with more extreme views, which are not representative of the views of most voters.

Some experts believe that open primaries reduce extremism because the candidates will try to appeal to voters with more moderate views, hoping to win votes from independents and even members of the other party. "Instead of appealing only to the extremes, candidates running for election in open primaries—where all candidates for an office appear on the same ballot—must tailor their message to appeal to centrists and even voters from the opposing party,"[35] explains Jason Altmire, a former US representative from Pennsylvania who has written a book about political polarization in America.

There is some evidence indicating that open primaries produce more moderate elected officials. A 2020 study conducted by the University of Southern California found that open primaries produced less extreme lawmakers in Congress. The study also found that top-two primaries—where the top two candidates with the most votes, regardless of party, advance to the general election—produce even less extreme legislators. As of June 2021, California, Louisiana, and Washington used top-two primaries. "Advocates for reform argue that top-two primary creates incentives for legislators to be less extreme than those elected in closed primary systems, as they must appeal to same-party, different-party, and independent voters,"[36] says Christian Grose, academic director of the University of Southern California Schwarzenegger Institute for State and Global Policy and author of the study.

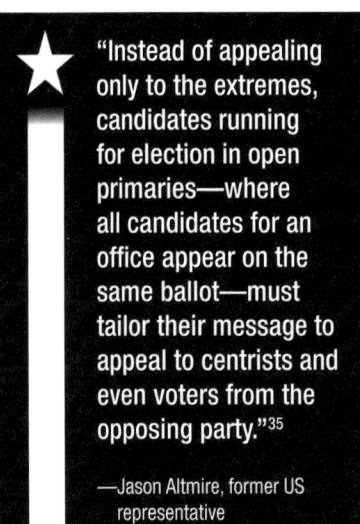

"Instead of appealing only to the extremes, candidates running for election in open primaries—where all candidates for an office appear on the same ballot—must tailor their message to appeal to centrists and even voters from the opposing party."[35]

—Jason Altmire, former US representative

Citizens' Assemblies

Another proposed solution to the wide divide between Americans is to encourage people to talk about important issues instead of politics. Citizens' assemblies are one way of doing this. In these assemblies, representative citizens gather to deliberate difficult social or political issues. The members then recommend policy solutions to policy makers.

Since 2016, Ireland has used citizens' assemblies to debate important issues. Ireland's first Citizens' Assembly was composed of one chairperson and ninety-nine citizens who were randomly selected to be representative of Ireland's population. They met for twelve weekends and heard from experts on five issues, including climate change. The members of the assembly had time to debate and consider proposed policy recommendations to address the issues. Over 80 percent of the members voted in support of the policy recommendations to address climate change, suggesting that a diverse group of people can reach a consensus on tough issues. Ireland has since used citizens' assemblies to debate other issues, such as gender equality.

However, some political scientists do not believe that open primaries will significantly reduce polarization. Lee Drutman says that his review of studies on primaries did not show any connection between the type of primary process and extremism. Other scholars say that the impact of open primaries in reducing extremism is minimal. Marc Meredith, a political science professor at the University of Pennsylvania, says that with open primaries, "at best it's going to make a small dent in a mountain of polarization."[37]

Some voters prefer open primaries and think they can improve the political climate. According to a 2021 poll by John Zogby Strategies, 68 percent of voters in New York, which has closed primaries, think that open primaries could reduce hyperpartisanship. At a minimum, open primaries provide independent and third-party voters a say during the important primary process, which may increase the diversity of viewpoints beyond those of the two major parties.

Moving to a Multiparty System

The two-party system is often blamed for hyperpartisanship and polarization. Expanding the two-party system to a multiparty

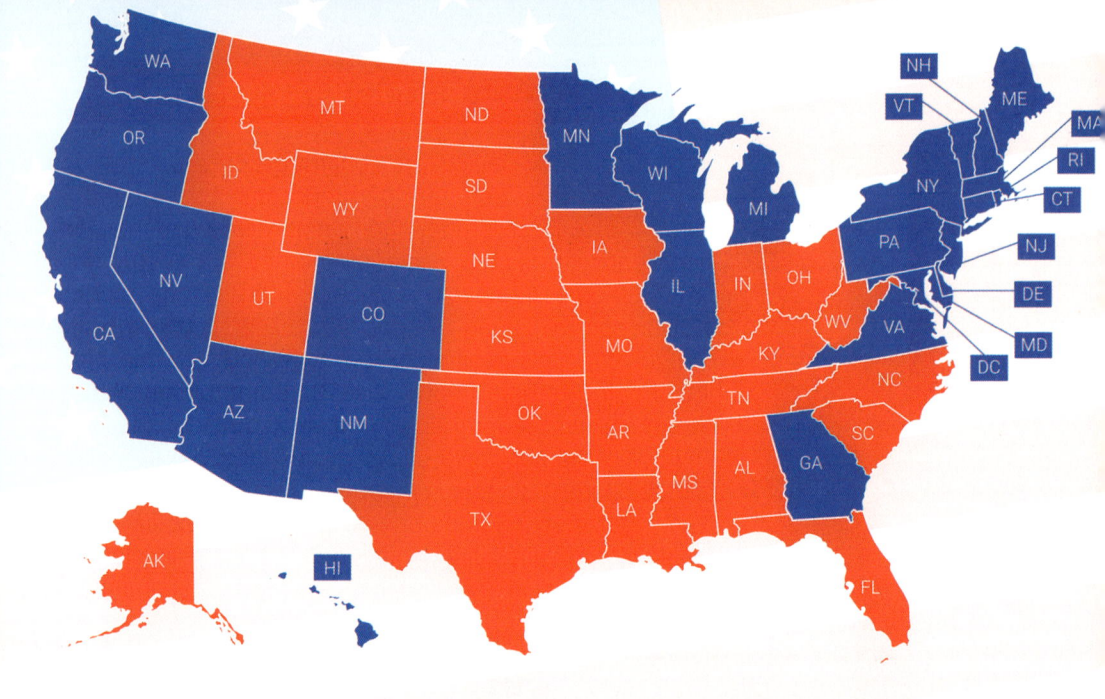

A 2020 election results map illustrates the control exerted on US politics by the two political parties—Democrats (blue) and Republicans (red). The two-party system is often blamed for hyperpartisanship and polarization.

system could reduce the bitter rivalries that currently plague American politics. A multiparty system means that multiple parties have a chance to gain control of the government, alone or in coalition with other parties. By having multiple parties compete for voters, competition increases, which is thought to promote better ideas and perhaps more civility between politicians. Because there would be more parties represented in legislative bodies, legislators would be encouraged to work with members of other parties to pass laws. In this context more viewpoints would be discussed, and compromise would be necessary between the various parties.

Some political scientists and commentators support a multiparty system. Drutman believes that having more parties is the answer to reducing polarization. Chuck Todd, moderator of NBC's *Meet the Press*, thinks a multiparty system of four major parties, created by splitting both major parties into two parties, would offer voters more choices and encourage legislative action by promoting coalitions. "If we condition politicians and the public to think that power requires [creating] coalitions (which a four-party system would likely institutionalize), then lo and behold, once in power, these folks would realize they have to create coalitions to pass legislation,"[38] says Todd.

Multimember Districts

American politics and election laws were designed around the existing two-party system, not a multiparty system. Thus, to create space for multiple parties, changes to the way elections are conducted would be necessary. One way to facilitate multiple parties is to change the way congressional representatives are elected. Currently, a single representative is elected to serve one congressional district, which is known as a single-member district. That means that one representative (who belongs to one party or is an independent) represents the views of the people in that district. An alternative to the single-member district is the multimember district. In a multimember district, multiple representatives (who likely belong to various parties) are elected to serve one district. A multimember district could be achieved by combining multiple existing districts into a larger district, which would be represented by multiple representatives.

Drutman supports moving to multimember districts to facilitate a multiparty system. Under his proposal for implementing such districts, if a party wins 40 percent of the votes in a state, then 40 percent of the state's congressional representatives would be from that party. The remaining representatives would be from other parties, similarly allocated based on the percentage of votes the parties received. As a result, one district would have representatives affiliated with

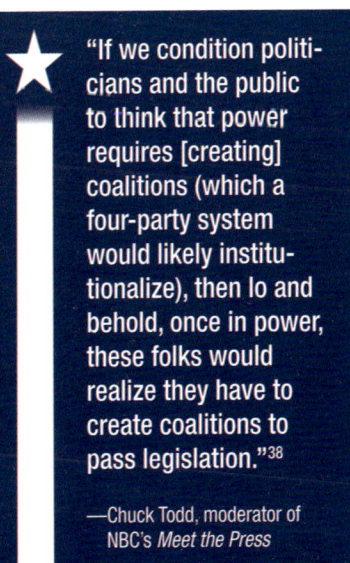

"If we condition politicians and the public to think that power requires [creating] coalitions (which a four-party system would likely institutionalize), then lo and behold, once in power, these folks would realize they have to create coalitions to pass legislation."[38]

—Chuck Todd, moderator of NBC's *Meet the Press*

Fixing Social Media

Social media has been blamed for fueling polarization, particularly by promoting disinformation and extremism. Although social media did not create polarization, the algorithms of social media platforms play a key role in increasing it. For example, Facebook's algorithm "rewards posts that provoke the most extreme reactions—often anger, rage or fear—because it was designed to keep users looking at the platform for as long as possible, no matter how it makes them feel or what it makes them think," says *Time* magazine correspondent Charlotte Alter.

Former Facebook employee Frances Haugen testified before Congress in 2021 and suggested that fixing the algorithm could reduce the promotion of shocking posts, which could reduce the spread of content designed to divide Americans. Haugen recommended that the law be reformed to hold social media platforms liable for content posted on their sites, which could prompt the platforms to change their algorithms.

Charlotte Alter, "How Fixing Facebook's Algorithm Could Help Teens—and Democracy," *Time*, October 5, 2021. https://time.com.

---

different parties. Multimember districts avoid the winner-take-all scenario currently in place, wherein the candidate with the most votes wins the election. This could also work for state legislatures.

Multimember districts may increase voter turnout because even voters who support candidates from the minority party or third parties would have a shot at electing a representative. For example, if a Democrat lived in a single-member district that always elects a Republican, that voter might not vote because the district has little chance of electing a Democrat. In other words, the voter may feel like casting his or her vote is unimportant. However, if that voter lived in a multimember district, the voter may be more likely to vote because some percentage of the representatives would be Democrats.

Ranked Voting

Another way to encourage multiple parties is to change the way voters cast their votes. In most places across the United States, voters cast a vote for one candidate in each race. They select one candidate for each office, such as president, US representative, US senator, and so on. However, there are other voting methods. Ranked voting, which is also known as instant runoff voting, is one example that has been implemented in Maine and some cities across the United States. Instead of simply casting a vote for one candidate, voters rank the candidates, indicating their choices for first, second, third, fourth, and so on. If the voter's first-choice candidate does not receive enough votes to win the election, the voter's second- and third-choice votes may be counted. The idea of ranked voting is that voters have more say and that the candidate with the most overall support wins.

The tallying of ranked voting is somewhat complicated. After tallying first-choice votes, if one candidate receives a majority of the votes (50 percent plus one vote), that candidate is deemed the winner. If no candidate earns a majority of the votes, the candidate with the fewest number of first-choice votes is eliminated. On ballots where the first-choice candidate is eliminated, the second-choice vote is counted as the vote. Based on the new tally, if one

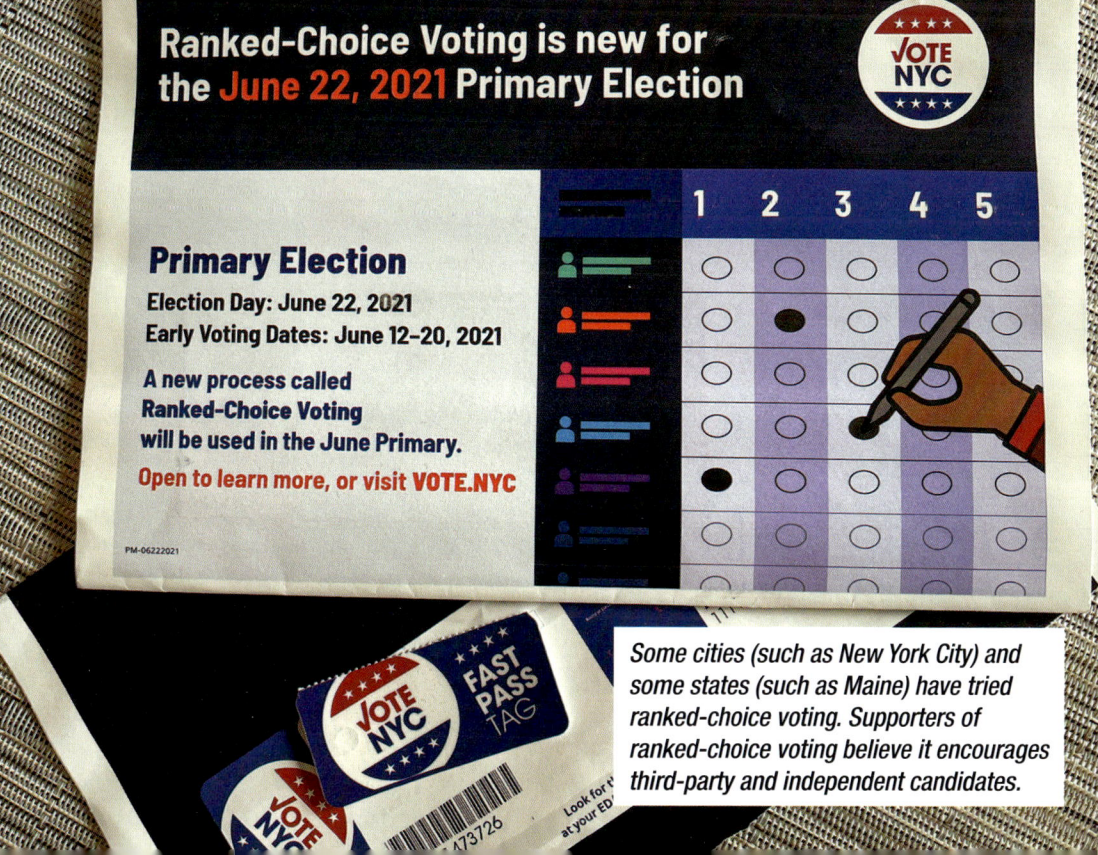

Some cities (such as New York City) and some states (such as Maine) have tried ranked-choice voting. Supporters of ranked-choice voting believe it encourages third-party and independent candidates.

candidate receives a majority of the votes, that candidate wins. If not, the process is repeated until one candidate wins a majority. Some opponents of ranked voting say that this process is confusing to voters. They also claim that voters may not trust election outcomes given that computers redistribute votes, making it harder for outside groups to confirm that the votes were counted accurately.

Proponents of ranked voting believe that it encourages third-party and independent candidates. To ensure that their vote makes a difference, sometimes voters vote for a major-party candidate even though they favor a third-party candidate. With ranked voting, voters may be more willing to vote for their favorite candidate, such as a third-party candidate, instead of voting strategically. That is because, even if a voter's top choice does not win, the second-choice vote may be tallied if no candidate wins enough first-choice votes. Proponents believe that ranked voting increases the chances of third-party and independent candidates winning elections.

Proponents also believe that ranked voting produces more civil elections and better policy debate. Given that second-place (or even lower ranked) votes may determine the outcome of elections, candidates are more likely to try to appeal to more people. In doing so, candidates may forgo personal attacks on other candidates to avoid alienating voters. The Committee for Ranked Choice Voting explains, "You are less likely to rank as your second choice a candidate who has issued personal attacks against your favorite candidate."[39] As a result, candidates may focus the debate on policy issues, not personal attacks.

Finding Ways to Work Together

A combination of reforms is likely needed to reduce hyperpartisanship and polarization in America. In addition to changing the systems that govern politics and elections, ordinary Americans can change how they speak to each other and seek to identify shared values and beliefs. To protect democracy, defeat enemies, and solve complex issues such as climate change, Americans are going to have to find a way to work together.

SOURCE NOTES

Introduction: The Pandemic Highlights a Divided Nation

1. Quoted in *New York Times*, "Read President Trump's Speech on Coronavirus Pandemic: Full Transcript," March 11, 2020. www.nytimes.com.
2. Jonathan Rothwell and Christos Makridis, "Politics Is Wrecking America's Pandemic Response," Brookings Institution, September 17, 2020. www.brookings.edu.

Chapter One: Political Parties in the United States

3. Quoted in Sarah Pruitt, "The Founding Fathers Feared Political Factions Would Tear the Nation Apart," History.com, March 7, 2019. www.history.com.
4. Quoted in Lee Drutman, "America Is Now the Divided Republic the Framers Feared," *The Atlantic*, January 2, 2020. www.theatlantic.com.
5. George Washington, "Washington's Farewell Address to the People of the United States," US Senate. www.senate.gov.
6. Jennifer Victor, "The Dangers of Partisan Animosity," Vox, April 3, 2017. www.vox.com.
7. Didi Kuo, "Challenges to Parties in the United States and Beyond," Vox, June 20, 2019. www.vox.com.
8. Nate Cohn, "Why Rising Diversity Might Not Help Democrats as Much as They Hope," *New York Times*, May 4, 2021. www.nytimes.com.

Chapter Two: Political Parties and Elections

9. Quoted in Ralph Nader, "Why Bernie Sanders Had to Run as a Democrat," *Chicago Tribune*, March 28, 2016. www.chicagotribune.com.
10. Nader, "Why Bernie Sanders Had to Run as a Democrat."
11. Quoted in Brian Faler, "Nader Scrambles to Collect Thousands of Signatures," *Washington Post*, April 3, 2004. www.washingtonpost.com.

12. Thomas E. Mann and Anthony Corrado, "Party Polarization and Campaign Finance," Brookings Institution, July 2014. www.brookings.edu.
13. Quoted in Michael Beckel, "Could Super PAC–Backed Third-Party Candidates Sway Presidential Race?," NBC News, August 31, 2012. www.nbcnews.com.
14. Harry Enten, "The Dangerous GOP Voting Laws Change Who Counts Votes," CNN, June 6, 2021. https://edition.cnn.com.
15. Joe Biden, "Remarks by President Biden on Protecting the Sacred, Constitutional Right to Vote," White House, July 13, 2021. www.whitehouse.gov.

Chapter Three: Gerrymandering to Create Election Advantage

16. Quoted in *Rucho v. Common Cause*, No. 18-422, 588 U.S. ___ (2019).
17. Quoted in *Rucho v. Common Cause*.
18. *Rucho v. Common Cause*.
19. Quoted in Steven Shepard, "Top Ohio Court Strikes Down State's Gerrymandered Congressional Map," Politico, January 14, 2022. www.politico.com.
20. Stephen Ohlemacher, "GOP Gerrymandering Creates Uphill Fight for Dems in the House," *PBS NewsHour*, March 31, 2014. www.pbs.org.
21. Julia Kirschenbaum and Michael Li, "Gerrymandering Explained," Brennan Center for Justice, August 10, 2021. www.brennancenter.org.
22. Quoted in Paul LeBlanc and Kelly Mena, "Obama Says GOP Gerrymandering Is 'Not How Democracy Is Supposed to Work,'" CNN, December 9, 2021. www.cnn.com.
23. Kirschenbaum and Li, "Gerrymandering Explained."

Chapter Four: Hyperpartisanship Threatens Democracy

24. Quoted in Alia E. Dastagir, "Election 2020: Terrified to Lose and Afraid to Hope," *USA Today*, October 28, 2020. www.usatoday.com.
25. Quoted in Thomas B. Edsall, "No Hate Left Behind," *New York Times*, March 13, 2019. www.nytimes.com.
26. Jennifer Victor, "The Dangers of Partisan Animosity," Vox, April 3, 2017. www.vox.com.

27. Quoted in Scott Detrow, "In Election's Final Weeks, Biden Makes a Case for Unity Amid a Tumultuous Time," NPR, October 6, 2020. www.npr.org.
28. Quoted in Susan Milligan, "How Partisan Politics Threatened Even Must-Pass Legislation in Congress," *U.S. News & World Report*, October 1, 2021. www.usnews.com.
29. Quoted in Thomas B. Edsall, "How to Tell When Your Country Is Past the Point of No Return," *New York Times*, December 15, 2021. www.nytimes.com.
30. Drutman, "We Need Political Parties. But Their Rabid Partisanship Could Destroy American Democracy," Vox, September 5, 2017. www.vox.com.
31. Drutman, "America Is Now the Divided Republic the Framers Feared."
32. Quoted in Edsall, "How to Tell When Your Country Is Past the Point of No Return."
33. Quoted in Kirsten Weir, "Why We Believe Alternative Facts," American Psychological Association, May 2017. www.apa.org.

Chapter Five: Reducing Polarization Between Parties and People

34. Pew Research Center, "Beyond Red vs. Blue: The Political Typology," November 9, 2021. www.pewresearch.org.
35. Jason Altmire, "Vote Down Your Crazy Uncle," *U.S. News & World Report*, November 24, 2017. www.usnews.com.
36. Quoted in Jenesse Miller, "Top-Two and Open Primary Elections Produce Less Extreme Lawmakers," USC News, May 14, 2020. https://news.usc.edu.
37. Quoted in Jonathan Lai, "Why Open Primary Elections Won't Solve Pa.'s Polarization Problem," *Philadelphia Inquirer*, May 31, 2018. www.inquirer.com.
38. Chuck Todd, "America's Two Major Political Parties Are Simply Too Big," MSNBC, August 3, 2021. www.msnbc.com.
39. Quoted in James Pollard, "What Is Ranked-Choice Voting and Where Is the System Used?," NBC San Diego, June 23, 2021. www.nbcsandiego.com.

FOR FURTHER RESEARCH

Books

Lee Drutman, *Breaking the Two-Party Doom Loop: The Case for Multiparty Democracy in America*. New York: Oxford University Press, 2020.

Ezra Klein, *Why We're Polarized*. New York: Simon & Schuster, 2020.

Steven Kornacki, *The Red and the Blue: The 1990s and the Birth of Political Tribalism*. New York: HarperCollins, 2018.

Internet Sources

Michael Dimock and Richard Wike, "America Is Exceptional in Its Political Divide," *Trust*, March 29, 2021. www.pewtrusts.org.

Yaffa Fredrick, "Welcome to the Fractured States of America," CNN, November 2019. https://edition.cnn.com.

Stephen Hawkins et al., "Hidden Tribes: A Study of America's Polarized Landscape," More in Common, 2018. https://hiddentribes.us.

Elaine Kamarck, "Voter Suppression or Voter Expansion? What's Happening and Does It Matter?," Brookings Institution, October 26, 2021. www.brookings.edu.

Michael Li et al., "Redistricting: A Mid-Cycle Assessment," Brennan Center for Justice, January 19, 2022. www.brennancenter.org.

Websites

Brennan Center for Justice
www.brennancenter.org
The Brennan Center for Justice is a nonpartisan law and policy institute that researches issues affecting democracy. The institute's website contains research reports and policy papers on current issues.

Democratic National Committee
https://democrats.org
The Democratic National Committee's website provides information about the Democratic Party and ways to get involved.

Green Party of the United States
www.gp.org
The Green Party's website provides information about the Green Party and ways to get involved.

Libertarian Party
www.lp.org
The Libertarian Party's website provides information about the Libertarian Party and ways to get involved.

Pew Research Center
www.pewresearch.org
The Pew Research Center is a nonpartisan research organization that conducts data-driven social science research, including public opinion polling and demographic research. Its website organizes research by topics, including Politics and Policy.

Republican National Committee
www.gop.com
The Republican National Committee's website provides information about the Republican Party and ways to get involved.

INDEX

Note: Boldface page numbers indicate illustrations.

abortion rights, 15, 16, 44
Abrams, Stacey, **22**
Adams, John, 9
Alter, Charlotte, 54
Altmire, Jason, 50
Anti-Federalists, 9–10

ballot access laws, 19–20
Biden, Joe, 21, 26, 41, 44
   infrastructure proposal of, 42
Brennan Center for Justice, 25, 60
Brookings Institution, 7

campaign finances, 21–24
citizens' assemblies, 51
Citizens Redistricting Commission (CA), 31
Cobb, David, 23–24
Cohn, Nate, 17
Committee for Ranked Choice Voting, 56
Congress, US
   executive orders bypassing, 44
   hyperpartisanship in, 41–43
   January 6 attack on, 38–39, **39**
   political coalitions in, 13
   See also redistricting
conservative/traditional ideologies, 15–16
Constitution, US, 9–10, 32
Corrado, Anthony, 23
COVID-19 pandemic, 42
   as challenge for federal government, 45
   changes in voting rules due to, 24
   political division over, 5–8

Democratic National Committee, 60
Democratic Party, 11, 15
   demographic characteristics of, 16
   election reforms favored by, 25–26
   2020 platform of, 14
Democratic-Republican Party, 10
Ditto, Peter, 47
Drutman, Lee, 43, 44, 45, 52, 53

early voting, 21
   in 2020 election, 24
elections, 2020 presidential
   spending on, 21
   turnout in, 24
Enten, Harry, 26
executive orders, 44

Facebook, 21, 54
Federalists, 9–10
Fern Hollow Bridge collapse (Pittsburgh), **42**
Freedom to Vote: John R. Lewis Act (proposed), 26

gerrymandering
   impact of technology on, 36
   political polarization and, 37

Ginsburg, Ruth Bader, 45
Great Depression, 15
Green Party, 11, 61
Grinnell College, 40
Grose, Christian, 50
gun control, 15, 16, 44

Hamilton, Alexander, 9
Haugen, Frances, 54

independent candidates
 ballot access and, 18, 19, 20
 funding and, 23
 ranked-choice voting and, 56

January 6 insurrection
 (Washington, DC, 2021),
 38–39, **39**
John Zogby Strategies, 51

Kapuscinski, Afton, 39–40
Kennedy School Institute of
 Politics (Harvard University), 4
Kirschenbaum, Julia, 34, 36
Klein, Ezra, 45
Kuo, Didi, 14

laissez faire capitalism, 15
Lancet, The (journal), 40
Levitt, Justin, 33–34
Li, Michael, 34, 36
liberal/progressive ideologies, 15
Libertarian Party, 11, 61
Louisiana State University, 41
Lussier, Danielle, 40

Macy, Michael W., 43
mail, voting by, 25
 in 2020 election, 24
Makridis, Christos, 8
Mann, Thomas E., 23, 43
McConnell, Mitch, 44–45
Meredith, Marc, 51

MIT Technology Review (journal), 21
multimember districts, 53–54
multiparty system, 51–53

Nader, Ralph, 18, 19, 20
National Conference of State
 Legislatures, 31
New Deal, 15
Newkirk, Vann R., II, 36
New York Times (newspaper), 46

Obama, Barack, 35
Ohlemacher, Stephen, 33
opinion polls. *See* surveys

party bosses, 27
party platforms, 14
Pew Research Center, 16, 40–41,
 47, 48, 61
political action committees
 (PACs), 23–24
political parties
 are important for healthy
  democracy, 12–14
 demographic characteristics of,
  16–17
 emergence of, 10–11
 goals/purposes of, 11–12
 impact of, on voting laws, 24
 platforms of, 14
 views of, on voting rights bill, 26
political polarization, 39–41
 gerrymandering and, 37
 partisan media and, 45
polls. *See* surveys
presidential nomination process,
 27
primary elections, 18
 closed versus open, 49–51
 party bosses replaced by, 27
Public Religion Research Institute,
 40

63

race, party affiliation and, 16, 35–36
ranked voting, 54–56, **55**
redistricting, 28–30
  commissions responsible for, 31
  gerrymandering and, 30–37
Republican National Committee, 61
Republican Party, 11, 15–16
  demographic characteristics of, 16
  election reforms favored by, 26
  2020 platform of, 14
Roberts, John, 29–30
Roosevelt, Franklin D., 15
Rothwell, Jonathan, 8
Ryan-Mosley, Tate, 21
Ryder, John, 36

Sanders, Bernie, 18, **19**
Scalia, Antonin, 44
Shapiro, Walter, 27
slavery, 15
social media, 13, 54
  voter turnout ads on, 21
Supreme Court, US, 44–45
  partisan redistricting and, 28, 29–30
  protesters at, **35**
surveys
  on attitudes toward opposing party members, 40–41
  of New York voters on open primaries, 51
  on political affiliations of Americans, 11
  on state of democracy in United States, 4
  on trust in federal government, 40

third parties/third-party candidates, 11
  ballot access and, 20
  campaign funding and, 22–23
  political action committees and, 23–24
  See also independent candidates
Todd, Chuck, 52–53
Trump, Donald, 5, 8, 14, 21
  alleges fraud in 2020 election, 24–25, 26
  bans travelers from Muslim countries, 44
  January 6 insurrection and, 38

United States, demographic trends in, 16–17
University of Maryland, 41

Victor, Jennifer, 12, 13
Virginia Public Access Project, 21
vote-counting laws, 26
voter ID laws, 25
voter turnout
  multimember districts and, 54
  social media ads encouraging, 21

Wang, Samuel, 36
Washington, George, 10, **10**
World Health Organization, 5